The Thinking Tree

Classical Fun-Schooling

LITERATURE AND POETRY COLLECTION

Level B - Elementary Level

FunSchoolingBooks.com

Literature from Public Domain
Dyslexie Font

TABLE OF CONTENTS

THE LITTLE THIEF IN THE PANTRY

Author Unknown

"Mother dear," said a little mouse one day, "I think the people in our house must be very kind; don't you? They leave such nice things for us in the pantry"

There was a twinkle in the mother's eye as she replied, "Well, my child, no doubt they are very well in their way, but I don't think they are quite as fond of us as you seem to think. Now remember, Greywhiskers, I have absolutely forbidden you to put your nose above the ground unless I am with you, for kind as the people are, I shouldn't be at all surprised if they tried to catch you."

Greywhiskers twitched his tail with scorn; he was quite sure he knew how to take care of himself, and he didn't mean to trot meekly after his mother's tail all his life. So as soon as she had curled herself up for an afternoon nap he stole away, and scampered across the pantry shelves.

Ah! Here was something particularly good today. A large iced cake stood far back upon the shelf, and Greywhiskers licked his lips as he sniffed it. Across the top of the cake there were words written in pink sugar; but as Greywhiskers could not read, he did not know that he was nibbling at little Miss Ethel's birthday cake.

He did feel a little guilty when he heard his mother calling. Off he ran, and was back in the nest again by the time his mother had finished rubbing her eyes after her nap.

She took Greywhiskers up to the pantry then, and when she saw the hole in the cake she seemed a little annoyed.

"Some mouse has evidently been here before us," she said, but of course she never guessed that it was her own little son.

The next day the naughty little mouse again popped up to the pantry when his mother was asleep but he could find nothing at all to eat, though there was a most delicious smell of toasted cheese. Soon he found a dear little wooden house, and there hung the cheese, just inside it. In ran Greywhiskers, but, oh! "click" went the little wooden house, and mousie was caught fast in a trap.

When morning came, the cook, who had set the trap, lifted it from the shelf and called a pretty little girl to come and see the thief who had eaten her cake. "What are you going to do with him?" asked Ethel.

"Why, drown him, my dear, to be sure" replied the cook as tears came into the little girl's eyes.

"You didn't know it was stealing, did you, mousie dear?" she asked.

"No," squeaked Greywhiskers sadly; "indeed I didn't."

When Cook's back was turned for a moment, tender-hearted little Ethel lifted the lid of the trap, and out popped mousie.

Oh! How quickly he ran home to his mother, and how she comforted and petted him until he began to forget his fright; and then she made him promise never to disobey her again, and you may be sure he never did.

THE END

Copy Your Favorite
Part of the Story Here:

What was the main point of this story?

Illustrate the story:

Draw your favorite character:

A SERIOUS QUESTION

Author Unknown

A kitten went a-walking
One morning in July,
And idly fell a-talking
With a great big butterfly.

The kitten's tone was airy,
The butterfly would scoff;
When there came along a fairy
Who whisked his wings right off.

And then—for it is written
Fairies can do such things—
Upon the startled kitten
She stuck the yellow wings.

The kitten felt a quiver,
She rose into the air,
Then flew down to the river
To view her image there.

With fear her heart was smitten,
And she began to cry,
"Am I a butter-kitten?
Or just a kitten-fly?"

Copy Your Favorite
Part of the Poem Here:

List your five favorite
Words from the poem:

_____

_____

_____

_____

_____

_____

Illustrate
the poem:

How does this
poem make you
feel?

THE WIND AND THE SUN

An Æsop's Fable

The Wind and the Sun were disputing which was the stronger. Suddenly they saw a traveler coming down the road, which gave the Sun an idea.

"I see a way to decide our dispute" said he. "Whichever of us can cause that traveler to take off his cloak shall be regarded as the stronger You begin."

So the Sun retired behind a cloud, and the Wind began to blow as hard as it could upon the traveler. But the harder he blew the more closely did the traveler wrap his cloak round him, till at last the Wind had to give up in despair.

Then the Sun came out and shone in all his glory upon the traveler, who soon

found it too hot to walk with his cloak on.

"KINDNESS IS MORE EFFECTIVE THAN SEVERITY."

Copy Your Favorite
Part of the Story Here:

What was the main point of this story?

Illustrate
the story:

Draw your
favorite character:

EDWARD LEAR'S NONSENSE LIMERICKS

There was an Old Man with a beard,
Who said, 'It is just as I feared!
Two Owls and a Hen,
Four Larks and a Wren,
Have all built their nests in my beard!'

Add the missing words:

There was an Old Man with a _____,
Who said, 'It is just as I _____!
Two _____ and a ____,
Four _____ and a _____,
Have all built their nests in my _____!'

There was a Young Lady whose eyes,
Were unique as to color and size;
When she opened them wide,
People all turned aside,
And started away in surprise.

There was a _____ Lady whose _____,
Were unique as to colour and _____;
When she _____ them _____,
People all _____ aside,
And started away in _____.

Copy Your Favorite
Part of the Poem Here:

List your five favorite
Words from the poem:

_____

_____

_____

_____

_____

Illustrate
the poem:

How does this
poem make you
feel?

ANDROCLES AND THE LION

An Aesop's Fable ~ Retold by James Baldwin

In Rome there was once a poor slave whose name was Androcles. His master was a cruel man, and so unkind to him that at last Androcles ran away.

He hid himself in a wild wood for many days; but there was no food to be found, and he grew so weak and sick that he thought he should die. So one day he crept into a cave and lay down, and soon he was fast asleep.

After a while a great noise woke him up. A lion had come into the cave, and was roaring loudly. Androcles was very much afraid, for he felt sure that the beast would kill him. Soon, however, he saw that the lion was not angry, but that he limped as though his foot hurt him.

Then Androcles grew so bold that he took hold of the lion's lame paw to see what was the matter. The lion stood quite still, and rubbed his head against the man's shoulder. He seemed to say, "I know that you will help me.

Androcles lifted the paw from the ground, and saw that it was a long, sharp thorn which hurt the lion so much. He took the end of the thorn in his fingers; then he gave a strong, quick pull, and out it came. The lion was full of joy. He jumped about like a dog, and licked the hands and feet of his new friend.

Androcles was not at all afraid after this; and when night came, he and the lion lay down and slept side by side. For a long time the lion brought food to Androcles every day; and the two became such good friends, that Androcles found his new life a very happy one.

One day some soldiers who were passing through the wood found Androcles in the cave. They knew who he was, and so took him back to Rome. It was the law at that time that every slave who ran away from his master should be made to fight a hungry lion. So a fierce lion was shut up for a while without food, and a time was set for the fight.

When the day came, thousands of people crowded to see the sport. They went to such places at that time very much as people now-a-days go to see a circus show or a game of baseball.

The door opened, and poor Androcles was brought in. He was almost dead with fear, for the roars of the lion could already be heard. He looked up, and saw that there was no pity in the thousands of faces around him. Then the hungry lion rushed in. With a single bound he reached the poor slave. Androcles gave a great cry, not of fear, but of gladness. It was his old friend, the lion of the cave.

The people, who had expected to see the man killed by the lion, were filled with wonder. They saw Androcles put his arms around the lion's neck; they saw the lion lie down at his feet, and lick them lovingly; they saw the great beast rub his head against the slave's face as though he wanted to be petted.

They could not understand what it all meant. After a while they asked Androcles to tell them about it. So he stood up before them, with his arm around the lion's neck, and told how he and the beast had lived together in the cave.

"I am a man but no man has ever befriended me. This poor lion alone has been kind to me; and we love each other as brothers."

The people were not so bad that they could be cruel to the poor slave now. "Live and be free!" they cried. "Let the lion go free too! Give both of them their liberty!"

And so Androcles was set free, and the lion was given to him for his own and they lived together in Rome for many years.

THE END

Copy Your Favorite
Part of the Story Here:

What was the main point of this story?

Illustrate
the story:

Draw your
favorite character:

THE MILKMAID AND HER PAIL

An Æsop's Fable

Patty the Milkmaid was going to market carrying her milk in a pail on her head. As she went along she began calculating what she would do with the money she would get for the milk.

"I'll buy some hens from Farmer Brown," said she, "and they will lay eggs each morning, which I will sell to the parson's wife. With the money that I get from the sale of those eggs I'll buy myself a lovely new frock and a fancy feathered hat; and when I go to market, everyone will admire my beauty! Polly Shaw will be quite jealous; but I don't care. I shall just look at her and toss my head like this." As she spoke she tossed her head back, the pail fell off it, and all the milk was spilt. So she had to go home and tell her mother what had occurred. "Ah, my child," said the mother,

"DO NOT COUNT YOUR CHICKENS BEFORE THEY ARE HATCHED."

Copy Your Favorite
Part of the Story Here:

_____

_____

_____

_____

_____

_____

_____

_____

_____

_____

_____

_____

What was the main point of this story?

Illustrate the story:

Draw your favorite character:

THE BROOM

Swish! swish! swish! swish!
A servant does my lady wish?
Here I hang against the wall,
Spruce and slender, straight and tall.
Take me down, and then, you know,
Swiftly to my work I'll go.

Steady, even strokes and strong!
So I sweep the dust along.
Throw the windows wide, that so
Out the dusky cloud may go.
Swish, and swish! now whirl away!
No more dust for us to-day!

In the corners now I rout,
Poking every atom out.
At the ceiling now I dash:
Lurking spiders feel my lash.
Cobweb, fly, and spider grey,
Out you come! away! away!

Swish, swee! swish, swee!
Sweeping is the game for me!
If, my little maid, you mean
Still to keep things neat and clean,
Trim and shining in your room,
Come to me, your friend the Broom!

Copy Your Favorite
Part of the Poem Here:

List your five favorite
Words from the poem:

_____
_____
_____
_____
_____

Illustrate
the poem:

How does this
poem make you
feel?

ABE LINCOLN GETS HIS CHANCE

Frances Cavanah

"Why did Pappy go so far away?" Sally asked one afternoon.

"When is he coming home?" asked Abe.

"Pretty soon, most likely."

Their mother, Nancy, laid down her sewing and tried to explain. Their Pa, Tom Lincoln, had had a hard time making a living for them. He was looking for a better farm. Tom was also a carpenter. Maybe some of the new settlers, who were going to Indiana to live, would give him work. Anyway, he thought that poor folks were better off up there.

Abe looked surprised. He had never thought about being poor. There were so many things that he liked to do in Kentucky. He liked to go swimming with Dennis after his chores were done. There were fish to be caught and caves to explore. He and Sally had had a chance to go to school for a few weeks. Abe could write his name, just like his father. He could read much better. Tom knew a few words, but his children could read whole sentences.

Abe leaned up against his mother.

"Tell us the story with our names," he begged. Nancy put her arm around him. She often told the children stories from the Bible. One of their favorites was about Abraham and Sarah.

"Now the Lord said unto Abraham," she began—and stopped to listen. The door opened, and Tom Lincoln stood grinning down at them.

"Well, folks," he said, "we're moving to Indiana."

Nancy and the children, taken by surprise, asked questions faster than Tom could answer them. He had staked out a claim about a hundred miles to the north, at a place called Pigeon Creek. He was buying the land from the government and could take his time to pay for it. He wanted to start for Indiana at once, before the weather got any colder.

Birthplace of Abraham Lincoln

It did not take long to get ready. A few possessions—a skillet, several pans, the water buckets, the fire shovel, clothes, a homespun blanket, a patchwork quilt, and several bearskins—were packed on the back of one of the horses. Nancy and Sally rode on the other horse. Abe and his father walked. At night they camped along the way.

When at last they reached the Ohio River, Abe stared in surprise. It was so blue, so wide, and so much bigger than the creek where he and Dennis had gone swimming. There were so many boats. One of them, a long low raft, was called a ferry. The Lincolns went right on board with their pack horses, and it carried them across the shining water to the wooded shores of Indiana.

Indiana was a much wilder place than Kentucky. There was no road leading

to Pigeon Creek; only a path through the forest. It was so narrow that some-

times Tom had to clear away some underbrush before they could go on. Or else

he had to stop to cut down a tree that stood in their way. Abe, who was big

and strong for his age, had his own little ax. He helped his father all he could.

Fourteen miles north of the river, they came to a cleared place in the for-

est. Tom called it his "farm." He hastily put up a shelter—a camp made of

poles and brush and leaves—where they could stay until he had time to build a

cabin. It had only three walls. The fourth side was left open, and in this open

space Tom built a fire.

The children helped their mother to unpack, and she mixed batter for cornbread in a big iron skillet. She cut up a squirrel that Tom had shot earlier in the day, and cooked it over the campfire. Nancy shivered. She knew that they had neighbors. Tom had told her there were seven other families living at Pigeon Creek. But the trees were so tall, the night so black, that she had a strange feeling that they were the only people alive for miles around.

"Don't you like it here, Mammy?" Abe asked. To him this camping out was an adventure, but he wanted his mother to like it, too.

"I'm just feeling a little cold," she told him.

"I like it," said Sally decidedly. "But it is sort of scary. Are you scared, Abe?"

"Me?" Abe stuck out his chest. "What is there to be scared of?"

At that moment a long-drawn-out howl came from the forest. Another seemed to come from just beyond their campfire. Then another and another, each howl louder and closer. The black curtain of the night was pierced by two green spots of light. The children huddled against their mother, but Tom Lincoln laughed.

"I reckon I know what you're scared of. A wolf."

"A wolf?" Sally shrieked.

"Yep. See its green eyes. But it won't come near our fire."

Tom got up and threw on another log. As the flames blazed higher, the green lights disappeared. There was a crashing sound in the underbrush.

"Hear him running away? Cowardly varmint!" Tom sat down again. "No wolf will hurt us if we keep our fire going."

Create Your Own Illustration

It was a busy winter. Abe worked side by side with his father. Tree after tree had to be cut down before crops could be planted. With the coming of spring, he helped his father to plow the stumpy ground. He learned to plow a straight furrow. He planted seeds in the furrows.

In the meantime, some of the neighbors helped Tom build a cabin. It had one room, with a tiny loft above. The floor was packed-down dirt. There were no windows. The only door was a long, up-and-down hole cut in one wall and covered by a bear-skin. But Tom had made a table and several three legged stools, and there was a pole bed in one corner. Abe's mother was glad to be living in a real house again, and she kept it neat and clean.

Nancy was no longer lonely. Aunt Betsy and her husband, Uncle Thomas, brought Dennis with them from Kentucky to live in the shelter near the Lincoln cabin. Several other new settlers arrived, settlers with children. A schoolmaster, Andrew Crawford, decided to start a school.

"Maybe you'll have a chance to go, Abe," Nancy told him. "You know what the schoolmaster down in Kentucky said. He said you were a learner."

Abe looked up at her and smiled. He was going to like living in Indiana!

THE END

Copy Your Favorite
Part of the Story Here:

What was the main point of this story?

Illustrate the story:

Draw your favorite character:

FOREIGN LANDS

Robert Louis Stevenson

Up into the cherry tree
Who should climb but little me?
I held the trunk with both my hands
And looked abroad on foreign lands.

I saw the next door garden lie,
Adorned with flowers, before my eye,
And many pleasant places more,
That I had never seen before.

I saw the dimpling river pass
And be the sky's blue looking-glass;
The dusty roads go up and down
With people tramping into town.

If I could find a higher tree
Farther and farther I should see,
To where the grown-up river slips
Into the sea among the ships.

To where the roads on either hand
Lead onward into fairy land,
Where all the children dine at five,
And all the playthings come alive.

Copy Your Favorite
Part of the Poem Here:

List your five favorite
Words from the poem:

_____

_____

_____

_____

_____

Illustrate
the poem:

How does this
poem make you
feel?

THE SHEPHERD BOY AND THE WOLF

An Æsop's Fable

There was once a young Shepherd Boy who tended his sheep at the foot of a mountain near a dark forest. It was rather lonely for him all day, so he thought upon a plan by which he could get a little company and some excitement. He rushed down towards the village calling out "Wolf, Wolf," and the villagers came out to meet him, and some of them stopped with him for a considerable time.

This pleased the boy so much that a few days afterwards he tried the same trick, and again the villagers came to his help. But shortly after this, a Wolf actually did come out from the forest, and began to worry the sheep, and the boy of course cried out "Wolf, Wolf," still louder than before. But this time, the villagers, who had been fooled twice before, thought the boy was again deceiving them, and nobody stirred to come to his help. So the Wolf made a good meal off the boy's flock, and when the boy complained, the wise man of the village said:

"A LIAR WILL NOT BE BELIEVED,

EVEN WHEN HE SPEAKS THE TRUTH."

Copy Your Favorite
Part of the Story Here:

What was the main point of this story?

Illustrate the story:

Draw your favorite character:

EDWARD LEAR'S NONSENSE LIMERICKS

There was a Young Lady whose bonnet,
Came untied when the birds sat upon it;
But she said: "I don't care!
All the birds in the air
Are welcome to sit on my bonnet!"

There was a Young Lady whose _____,
Came untied when the _____ sat upon it;
But she said: "I don't _____!
All the birds in the ____
Are _____ to sit on my _____!"

There was an Old Man in a tree,
Who was horribly bored by a Bee;
When they said, "Does it buzz?"
He replied, "Yes, it does!"
"It's a regular brute of a Bee!"

There was an ____ ____ in a tree,
Who was _____ bored by a Bee;
When they said, "Does it _____?"
He _____, "Yes, it does!"
"It's a _____ brute of a Bee!"

Copy Your Favorite
Part of the Poem Here:

_____

_____

_____

_____

_____

_____

_____

_____

_____

_____

_____

_____

List your five favorite
Words from the poem:

_____

_____

_____

_____

_____

Illustrate
the poem:

How does this
poem make you
feel?

SEA FEVER

John Masefield

I must go down to the seas again, to the lonely sea and the sky,
And all I ask is a tall ship and a star to steer her by;
And the wheel's kick and the wind's song and the white sail's shaking,
And a grey mist on the sea's face and a grey dawn breaking.

I must go down to the seas again, for the call of the running tide
Is a wild call and a clear call that may not be denied;
And all I ask is a windy day with the white clouds flying,
And the flung spray and the blown spume, and the sea-gulls crying.

I must go down to the seas again, to the vagrant gypsy life.
To the gull's way and the whale's way where the wind's like a whetted knife;
And all I ask is a merry yarn from a laughing fellow-rover,
And quiet sleep and a sweet dream when the long trick's over.

Draw the Sea:

Copy Your Favorite
Part of the Poem Here:

List your five favorite
Words from the poem:

_____

_____

_____

_____

_____

Illustrate
the poem:

How does this
poem make you
feel?

THE GOLDEN WINDOWS

Laura E. Richards

All day long a little boy worked hard, in field and barn and shed, for his people were poor farmers, and could not pay a workman; but at sunset there came an hour that was all his own, for his father had given it to him. Then, the boy would go up to the top of a hill and look across at another hill that rose some miles away. On this far hill stood a house with windows of clear gold and diamonds. They shone and blazed so that it made the boy wink to look at them: but after a while the people in the house put up shutters, as it seemed, and then it looked like any common farmhouse. The boy supposed they did this because it was supper-time; and then he would go into the house and have his supper of bread and milk, and so to bed.

One day, the boy's father called him and said, "You have been a good boy, and have earned a holiday. Take this day for your own, but remember that God gave it and try to learn some good thing."

The boy thanked his father and kissed his mother; then he put a piece of bread in his pocket, and started off to find the house with the golden windows.

It was pleasant walking. His bare feet made marks in the white dust, and when he looked back, the footprints seemed to be following him, and making company for him. His shadow, too, kept beside him, and would dance or run with him as he pleased; so it was very cheerful.

By and by he felt hungry; and he sat down by a brown brook that ran through the alder hedge by the roadside, and ate his bread, and drank the clear water. Then he scattered the crumbs for the birds, as his mother had taught him to do, and went on his way. After a long time he came to a high green hill; and when he had climbed the hill, there was the house on the top; but it seemed that the shutters were up, for he could not see the golden windows. When he came up to the house he could have wept, for the windows were made only of clear glass, like any others, and there was no gold anywhere about them.

A woman came to the door, and looked kindly at the boy, and asked him what he wanted. "I saw the golden windows from our hilltop," he said, "and I came to see them, but now they are only glass."

The woman shook her head and laughed. "We are poor farming people," she said, "and are not likely to have gold about our windows; but glass is better to see through."

She bade the boy sit down on the broad stone step at the door, and brought him a cup of milk, and a cake, and bade him rest; then she called her daughter, a child of his own age, and nodded kindly at the two, and went back to her work.

The little girl was barefooted like himself, and wore a brown cotton gown, but her hair was golden like the windows he had seen, and her eyes were blue like the sky at noon. She led the boy about the farm, and showed him her black calf with the white star on its forehead, and he told her about his own at home, which was red like a chestnut, with four white feet. Then, when they had eaten an apple together, and so had become friends, the boy asked her about the golden windows. The little girl nodded, and said she knew all about them, only he had mistaken the house.

"You have come quite the wrong way!" she said. "Come with me, and I will show you the house with the golden windows, and then you will see for yourself."

They went to a knoll that rose behind the farmhouse, and as they went the little girl told him that the golden windows could only be seen at a certain hour, about sunset.

"Yes, I know that!" said the boy.

When they reached the top of the knoll, the girl turned and pointed; and there on a hill far away stood a house with windows of clear gold and diamond, just as he had seen them. And when they looked again, the boy saw that it was his own home!

After this, he told the little girl that he must go; and he gave her his best

pebble, the white one with the red band, that he had carried for a year in his pocket.

She gave him three horse-chestnuts, one red like satin, one spotted, and one white

like milk. He promised to come again, but he did not tell her what he had learned;

and so he went back down the hill, and the little girl stood in the sunset light and

watched him.

The way home was long, it was dark before the boy reached his father's house;

but the lamplight and firelight shone through the windows, making them almost as

bright as he had seen them from the hilltop. When he opened the door, his mother

came to kiss him, his little sister ran to throw her arms about his neck, and his fa-

ther looked up and smiled from his seat by the fire.

"Have you had a good day?" asked his mother.

"And have you learned anything?" asked his father.

"Yes!" said the boy. "I have learned that our house has windows of gold and

diamond."

THE END

Copy Your Favorite
Part of the Story Here:

What was the main point of this story?

Illustrate
the story:

Draw your
favorite character:

THE FIELDMOUSE

Cecil Frances Alexander

Where the acorn tumbles down,
Where the ash tree sheds its berry,
With your fur so soft and brown,
With your eye so round and merry,
Scarcely moving the long grass,
Fieldmouse, I can see you pass.

Little thing, in what dark den,
Lie you all the winter sleeping?
Till warm weather comes again,
Then once more I see you peeping
Round about the tall tree roots,
Nibbling at their fallen fruits.

Fieldmouse, fieldmouse, do not go,
Where the farmer stacks his treasure,
Find the nut that falls below,
Eat the acorn at your pleasure,
But you must not steal the grain,
He has stacked with so much pain.

Make your hole where mosses spring,
Underneath the tall oak's shadow,
Pretty, quiet harmless thing,
Play about the sunny meadow.
Keep away from corn and house,
None will harm you, little mouse.

Copy Your Favorite
Part of the Poem Here:

List your five favorite
Words from the poem:

_____

_____

_____

_____

_____

Illustrate
the poem:

How does this
poem make you
feel?

OUR KITTENS

Evaleen Stein

Our kittens have the softest fur,
And the sweetest little purr,
And such little velvet paws
With such cunning little claws,
And blue eyes, just like the sky!
(Must they turn green, by and by?)
Two are striped like tigers, three
Are as black as black can be,
And they run so fast and play
With their tails, and are so gay,
Is it not a pity that
Each must grow into a cat?

OUR KITTENS

Evaleen Stein

Our kittens have the _____ fur,
And the _____ little purr,
And such little _____ paws
With such _____ little claws,
And blue _____, just like the sky!
(Must they turn _____, by and by?)
Two are _____ like tigers, three
Are as _____ as black can be,
And they run so _____ and play
With their _____, and are so gay,
Is it not a _____ that
Each must _____ into a cat?

**Copy Your Favorite
Part of the Poem Here:**

List your five favorite
Words from the poem:

_____

_____

_____

_____

_____

Illustrate
the poem:

How does this
poem make you
feel?

A CHILD'S BIOGRAPHY

Louisa May Alcott

More than 100 years ago in the city of Boston, there lived a small girl who had the naughty habit of running away. On a certain April morning, almost as soon as her mother finished buttoning her dress, Louisa May Alcott slipped out of the house and up the street as fast as her feet could carry her.

Louisa crept through a narrow alley and crossed several streets. It was a beautiful day, and she did not care so very much just where she went, so long as she was having an adventure, all by herself. Suddenly, she came upon some children who said they were going to a nice, tall ash heap to play. They asked her to join them.

Louisa thought they were fine playmates, for when she grew hungry, they shared some cold potatoes and bread crusts with her. She would not have thought this much of a lunch in her mother's dining-room, but for an outdoor picnic, it did very well.

When she tired of the ash heap, she bade the children good-by, thanked them for their kindness, and hop-skipped to the Common, where she must have wandered about for hours, because, all of a sudden, it began to grow dark. Then she wanted to get home. She wanted her doll, her kitty, and her mother! It frightened her when she could not find any street that looked natural. She was hungry and tired, too.

She threw herself down on some door-steps to rest and to watch the lamp-lighter, for you must remember this was long before there was any gas or electricity in Boston. At this moment a big dog came along. He kissed her face and hands and then sat down beside her with a sober look in his eyes, as if he were thinking: "I guess, Little Girl, you need some one to take care of you!"

Poor tired Louisa leaned against his neck and was fast asleep in no time. The dog kept very still. He did not want to wake her.

Pretty soon, the town crier went by. He was ringing a bell and reading in a loud voice, from a paper in his hand, the description of a lost child. You see, Louisa's father and mother had missed her early in the forenoon and had looked for her in every place they could think of. Each hour they grew more worried, and at dusk they decided to hire this man to search the city.

When the runaway woke up and heard what the man was shouting—"Lost— Lost—A little girl, six years old, in a pink frock, white hat, and new, green shoes"— she called out in the darkness: "Why—dat's ME!"
The town crier took Louisa by the hand and led her home, where you may be sure she was welcomed with joy.

Mr. and Mrs. Alcott, from first to last, had had a good many frights about this flyaway Louisa. Once, when she was only two years old they were traveling with her on a steamboat, and she darted away, in some moment when no one was noticing her, and crawled into the engine-room to watch the machinery. Of course her clothes were all grease and dirt, and she might have been caught in the machinery and hurt.

You won't be surprised to know that the next day after this last affair, Louisa's parents made sure that she did not leave the house. Indeed, to be entirely certain of her whereabouts, they tied her to the leg of a big sofa for a whole day!

Except for this one fault, Louisa was a good child, so she felt much ashamed that she had caused her mother, whom she loved dearly, so much worry. As she sat there, tied to the sofa, she made up her mind that she would never frighten her so again. No—she would cure herself of the running-away habit!

After that day, whenever she felt the least desire to slip out of the house without asking permission, she would hurry to her own little room and shut the door tight. To keep her mind from bad plans, she would shut her eyes and make up stories—think them all out, herself, you know. Then, when some of them seemed pretty good, she would write them down so that she would not forget them. By and by she found she liked making stories better than anything she had ever done in her life.

Her mother sometimes wondered why Louisa grew so fond of staying in her little chamber at the head of the stairs, all of a sudden, but was pleased that the runaway child had changed into such a quiet, like-to-stay-at-home girl.

It was a long time before Louisa dared to mention the stories and rhymes she had hidden in her desk, but finally she told her mother about them, and when Mrs. Alcott had read them, she advised her to keep on writing. Louisa did so and became one of the best American story-tellers. She wrote a number of books, and if you begin with Lulu's Library, you will want to read Little Men and Little Women and all the books that dear Louisa Alcott ever wrote. At first Louisa was paid but small sums for her writings, and as the Alcott family were poor, she taught school, did sewing, took care of children, or worked at anything, always with a merry smile, so long as it provided comforts for those she loved.

When the Civil War broke out, she was anxious to do something to help, so she went into one of the Union hospitals as a nurse. She worked so hard that she grew very ill, and her father had to go after her and bring her home. One of her books tells about her life in the hospital.

It was soon after her return home that her books began to sell so well that she found herself, for the first time in her life, with a great deal of money.

There was enough to buy luxuries for the Alcott family—there was enough for her to travel. No doubt she got more happiness in traveling than some people, for she found boys and girls in England, France, and Germany reading the very books she herself, Louisa May Alcott, had written.

Then, too, at the age of fifty, she enjoyed venturing into new places just as well as she did the morning she sallied forth to Boston Common in her new green shoes!

THE END

Copy Your Favorite
Part of the Story Here:

What was the main point of this story?

Illustrate
the story:

Draw your
favorite character:

DID YOU EVER?

Evaleen Stien

Did you ever see a fairy in a rose-leaf coat and cap
Swinging in a cobweb hammock as he napped his noonday nap?
Did you ever see one waken very thirsty and drink up
All the honey-dew that glimmered in a golden buttercup?
Did you ever see one fly away on rainbow-twinkling wings?
If you did not, why, how comes it that you never see such things?

DID YOU EVER?

Evaleen Stien

Did you ever see a _____ in a rose-leaf coat and cap
Swinging in a cobweb _____ as he napped his _____ nap?
Did you ever see one waken very _____ and drink up
All the honey-dew that _____ in a _____ buttercup?
Did you ever see one fly away on _____-twinkling wings?
If you did not, why, how _____ it that you _____ see such things?

Draw a Fairy

WRITE YOUR OWN
STORIES & POEMS

MY STORY

MY STORY

MY ILLUSTRATION

MY ILLUSTRATION

MY POEM

MY ILLUSTRATION

MY STORY

MY ILLUSTRATION

MY STORY

MY ILLUSTRATION

MY POEM

MY ILLUSTRATION

MY POEM

MY ILLUSTRATION

The Thinking Tree

FunSchoolingBooks.com

Made in the USA
Las Vegas, NV
11 August 2023

75965900R00059